HALLOWEEN JOKES

FUN HALLOWEEN JOKES AND RIDDLES FOR KIDS, ENTERTAINMENT AND GIGGLES!

CHARLOTTE GIBBS

SPECIAL BONUS!

Want These 2 Books For FREE?

 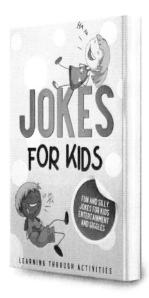

Get **FREE**, unlimited access to these and all of our new kids books by joining our community!

Scan W/ Your Camera To Join!

TABLE OF CONTENTS

LET'S GROW TOGETHER!

We Would Really Appreciate It If You Could Take A Moment To Leave Us A Review On Amazon!

INTRODUCTION: WHAT IS HALLOWEEN?

PUMPKINS, CANDY, COSTUMES, AND WEATHER CHANGES...

Just as the summer heat, long school vacation, and fireworks of Independence Day come to a close and everyone is down about being back in class, here comes Halloween!

As Halloween approaches, the world begins to change. After a long and hot summer, we are greeted with harvests, colorful leaves, cool weather, and oh-so-much candy and chocolate.

There are many different reasons to celebrate Halloween. For example, Christians celebrate Halloween as it is the time of year when their saints and lost loved ones are praised, and generally celebrated. Others celebrate Halloween as it is a sign that the harvest season is coming to a close and a dreary winter is about to start.

Halloween is the one holiday every year that is covered with spooky colored decorations and candies. Everything is covered in oranges, reds, yellows, blacks, and purples—from holiday lights, to wreaths, to candy.

To keep in the fashion of this darkly colored holiday, here is a book filled with funny and punny Halloween jokes and riddles that your kids, and you, will love!

This book includes seven chapters, each with its own spooky joke and creepy theme.

HALLOWEEN JOKES
FUN HALLOWEEN JOKES AND RIDDLES FOR KIDS, ENTERTAINMENT AND GIGGLES!

2

KNEE-KNOCKING KNOCK KNOCK JOKES
Knock, knock.
Who's there?
Scary Funny Jokes.
Scary Funny Jokes who?
There are scary funny jokes in this chapter!

THE PUNNY FUNNY SKELETONY
These jokes are downright bone-chilling!

TANTALIZING TARANTULA TONGUE TWISTERS
We bet you can't say them really fast ten times! But you can try.

CLASSIC AND FUNNY QUESTION AND ANSWER HALLOWEEN JOKES
Question: What do you call a good skeleton joke?
Answer: A funny bone!

RIDICULOUS AND SPOOKY RIDDLES
Questions that are short and sweet, like: "What's an animal with four feet?"
Answer us, we beg of you, making you think is what we do. What are we?
Riddles!

FUN FACTS ABOUT HALLOWEEN
Did you know there is a lot more to Halloween than meets the eye?
Fun and Creepy Halloween Poems

We've collected for this chapter some of the creepiest, spookiest, and most fun poems to set the mood for Halloween night!

With that being said, we hope you enjoy this absolutely hair-raising book of Halloween puns and jokes!

HALLOWEEN JOKES
FUN HALLOWEEN JOKES AND RIDDLES FOR KIDS, ENTERTAINMENT AND GIGGLES!

3

CHAPTER 1
KNOCK KNOCK JOKES

Knock, knock.
Who's there?
Phillip!
Phillip who?
Phillip my Halloween bag, please!

Knock, knock.
Who's there?
Ivana!
Ivana who?
Ivana get a lot of candy tonight!

Knock, knock.
Who's there?
Tricker!
Tricker who?
Tricker treat, give me something good to eat!

Knock, knock.
Who's there?
Frankie!
Frankie who?
Frankie Stein!

Knock, knock.
Who's there?
Witch!
Witch who?
Witch of you has all the Halloween candy?

Knock, knock.
Who's there?
Witch!
Witch who?
Witch of you stole my lucky broomstick?

Knock, knock.
Who's there?
Boo!
Boo who?
Oh, don't cry! It was only a joke.

Knock, knock.
Who's there?
Jackal!
Jackal who?
Jackal lantern!

Knock, knock!
Who's there?
Howl!
Howl who?
Howl you ever know unless you open up the door?

Knock, knock.
Who's there?
Jackal!
Jackal who?
Jackal and Mr. Hyde!

Knock, knock.
Who's there?
Cement!
Cement who?
**Cement to scream when she saw
the monster but she passed out
instead!**

KNOCK, KNOCK.
WHO'S THERE?
GETYUR!
GETYUR WHO?
GETYUR HANDS OUT OF MY
CANDY BAG!

HALLOWEEN JOKES
FUN HALLOWEEN JOKES AND RIDDLES FOR KIDS, ENTERTAINMENT AND GIGGLES!

5

Knock, knock.
Who's there?
Ben!
Ben who?
Ben waiting all year for Halloween treats!

Knock, knock.
Who's there?
Ooze!
Ooze who?
Ooze are you?

Knock, knock.
Who's there?
Judo!
Judo who?
Judo know how much I love candy!?

Knock, knock.
Who's there?
Fangs!
Fangs who?
Fangs for all the candy!

KNOCK, KNOCK.
WHO'S THERE?
GHOST!
GHOST WHO?
GHOSTS DON'T
KNOCK. GO AWAY!

HALLOWEEN JOKES
FUN HALLOWEEN JOKES AND RIDDLES FOR KIDS, ENTERTAINMENT AND GIGGLES!

6

Knock, knock.
Who's there?
Orange!
Orange who?
Orange you going to carve your jack-o'- lantern?

Knock, knock.
Who's there?
Dishes!
Dishes who?
Dishes the best Halloween party ever!

Knock, knock.
Who's there?
Olive!
Olive who?
Olive candy corn so much!

Knock, knock.
Who's there?
Ice cream!
Ice cream who?
Ice cream at spooky, scary masks!

Knock, knock.
Who's there?
Twik!
Twik who?
Twik or treat, give me candy!

Knock, knock.
Who's there?
Wanda!
Wanda who?
Wanda which house has the best candy this year?

KNOCK, KNOCK.
WHO'S THERE?
WANDA!
WANDA WHO?
WANDA BE THE
WEREWOLF OR THE
ZOMBIE?

Knock, knock.
Who's there?
Canoe!
Canoe who?
Canoe help me zip up my
Halloween costume?

Knock, knock.
Who's there?
Wooden shoe!
Wooden shoe who?
Wooden shoe like to go to the
pumpkin patch with me?

Knock, knock.
Who's there?
Hans!
Hans who?
Hans off my spooky mask!

Knock, knock.
Who's there?
Figs!
Figs who?
Figs your own mask!

KNOCK, KNOCK.
WHO'S THERE?
BEE!
BEE WHO?
BEE-WARE, YOU'RE IN
FOR A SCARE!

HALLOWEEN JOKES
FUN HALLOWEEN JOKES AND RIDDLES FOR KIDS, ENTERTAINMENT AND GIGGLES!

8

Knock, knock.
Who's there?
Diane!
Diane who?
Diane to go trick or treating
tonight!

Knock, knock.
Who's there?
Aida!
Aida who?
Aida small dinner so I have room
for more candy!

Knock, knock.
Who's there?
Abbot!
Abbot who?
Abbot time to go trick or
treating!

Knock, knock.
Who's there?
Butter!
Butter who?
Butter give me lots of candy!

Knock, knock.
Who's there?
Al!
Al who?
Al trade you my apple for that
tootsie roll!

Knock, knock.
Who's there?
Doughnut!
Doughnut who?
Doughnut forget to light the jack-
o'-lantern!

Knock, knock.
Who's there?
Doughnut!
Doughnut who?
Doughnut be sad, it's Halloween!

Knock, knock.
Who's there?
Howie!
Howie who?
Howie going to scare the kiddies
on Halloween?

Knock, knock.
Who's there?
Howie!
Howie who?
Howie going to celebrate
Halloween this year?

Knock, knock.
Who's there?
Imogen!
Imogen who?
Imogen a world without trick or
treating?

Knock, knock.
Who's there?
Hugo!
Hugo who?
Hugo put your costume on. Quick!

Knock, knock.
Who's there?
Turin!
Turin who?
Turin to a zombie if you get bit!

Knock, knock.
Who's there?

Goat!
Goat who?
Goat to that haunted house and knock on the door!

Knock, knock.
Who's there?
Thermos!
Thermos who?
Thermos be some better candy around here!

Knock, knock.
Who's there?
Thad!
Thad who?
Thad house creeps me out!

KNOCK, KNOCK.
WHO'S THERE?
LETTUCE!
LETTUCE WHO?
LETTUCE IN! WE WANT CANDY!

HALLOWEEN JOKES
FUN HALLOWEEN JOKES AND RIDDLES FOR KIDS, ENTERTAINMENT AND GIGGLES!

10

Knock, knock.
Who's there?
Disguise!
Disguise who?
Disguise excited for Halloween night!

Knock, knock.
Who's there?
Dustin!
Dustin who?
Dustin off the cobwebs from last Halloween's costume!

Knock, knock.
Who's there?
Earl!
Earl who?
Earl be happy once we get some candy!

Knock, knock.
Who's there?
Zoom!
Zoom who?
Zoom else would it be?

KNOCK, KNOCK.
WHO'S THERE?
ESSEN!
ESSEN WHO?
ESSEN IT BEEN FUN
READING THESE
HALLOWEEN JOKES?

HALLOWEEN JOKES
FUN HALLOWEEN JOKES AND RIDDLES FOR KIDS, ENTERTAINMENT AND GIGGLES!

CHAPTER 2
FUNNY PUNS

Why did the werewolf bite the skeleton's arm?

Because it was humerus to him!

What did the boogeyman name his horse?

Night-mare!

HOW DOES A WOLF SAY HALLOWEEN?

HOWLOWEEN!

HALLOWEEN JOKES
FUN HALLOWEEN JOKES AND RIDDLES FOR KIDS, ENTERTAINMENT AND GIGGLES!

12

What do monsters have for a snack?
Deviled eggs!

Where do zombies go swimming?
In the Dead Sea!

Where is the witch's temple?
In front of their ears and behind their eyes!

Why'd the werewolf have to take a bath after swallowing a clock?
He had ticks!

How do you make a witch itch?
Drop the w!

WHY DOESN'T THE MUMMY ANSWER THE PHONE?

HE'S A LITTLE WRAPPED UP AT THE MOMENT!

Where did the ghost pirates park their ship before trick or treating?

In the pARRRRking lot!

Why was the vampire circus clown's lips red?

He just ate from the jugular!

How does the ghost get around the city?

On a boocycle!

What did the scarecrow say to the trick or treater dressed up as a crow?

Boo!

WHEN DOES A JACK-O-LANTERN EAT?

WHENEVER YOU CARVE OUT ITS MOUTH!

HALLOWEEN JOKES
FUN HALLOWEEN JOKES AND RIDDLES FOR KIDS, ENTERTAINMENT AND GIGGLES!

14

What do pumpkins eat at the movies?
Pulp corn!

What is a monster's favorite dessert?
I-scream!

What do you call a fat jack-o'-lantern?
A plumpkin!

Why are vampires easy to fool?
They're suckers!

Where do ghosts go for vacation?
Mali-boo!

How do you say bye to a vampire?
So long, sucker!

Why did the ghost go to the bar?
For the boos!

Why are ghosts good cheerleaders?
They have high spirits!

What happens when you drop a pumpkin?
It turns into a squash!

WHY IS IT BAD TO BE KISSED BY A VAMPIRE?

IT'S A PAIN IN THE NECK!

Why shouldn't you trust someone who gives you Cheerios on Halloween?
They could be a cereal killer!

What did the werewolf say after dinner?
Fangs for the food!

What is a vampire's favorite holiday?
Fangs-giving!

Why didn't Bobby wear the skeleton costume?
He wanted everyone to know he had guts!

Where do spirits get their food?
At the ghostery store!

How do you fix a leaking jack-o'-lantern?
With a pumpkin patch!

What did the pumpkin say at the Halloween party?
I'm just here for a gourd time!

What happened to the vampire after too many Halloween puns?
He went batty!

WHERE DID THE RICH GHOST GET HER CLOTHES?

AT THE BOO-TIQUE!

What did one pumpkin say to the pumpkin that stole its candy?
Don't be a jerk-o'-lantern!

What did Dracula say to his admirers?
You should join my fang club!

Why did the ghost eat so much candy?
The sugar was just eerie-sistible!

What type of fruit do vampires love?
Neck-tarines

How did the witch escape after robbing a bank?
Riding her broom gave her a clean getaway!

Who did the monster marry?
His ghoul friend!

Why was the ghost lonely?
Because he had no body!

What did the ghost driver say to his passengers?
Fasten your sheet-belts!

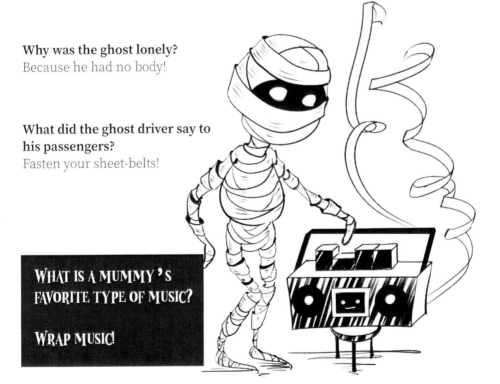

WHAT IS A MUMMY'S FAVORITE TYPE OF MUSIC?

WRAP MUSIC!

Why does Dracula use mouthwash?

He has bat breath!

What did the ghost say to the lying skeleton?

I can see right through you!

Why can't a mummy relax?

He's afraid to unwind!

What did the skeleton say before serving dinner?

Bone appetit!

HALLOWEEN JOKES
FUN HALLOWEEN JOKES AND RIDDLES FOR KIDS, ENTERTAINMENT AND GIGGLES!

18

CHAPTER 3
TONGUE TWISTERS

Which watchful witch wants which sandwich?

Creepy crawly critters crawl across crustaceans.

Trick-or-treat for something sweet. Stop the trick-or-treat trick before I get sick.

Sweet the trick-or-treat treat I want to eat. Trick or treat, I repeat.

Creepy crawling critters crawl carelessly through crazy creepy corridors.

Seven spindly spiders spin spooky silk speedily.

Crazy children crave candy wearing chilling costumes.

If big black bats could blow bubbles, how big of bubbles would big black bats blow?

Scary scarred scarecrows stared scarily.

GROUPS OF GREEDY GREEN GOBLINS GRAB AT GREEN, GROANING GHOSTS.

Seven spindly spiders spin spooky silk speedily.

Giant, gross, green ghouls giggle at ghosts.

Don't buy big black cats or blind bats' blood.

Mr. Mummy mustn't mess up Mrs. Mummy's marvelous make-up.

No nose knows like a Gnome's nose knows.

Helen hardly ever heard the horrible haunted house's Halloween howl.

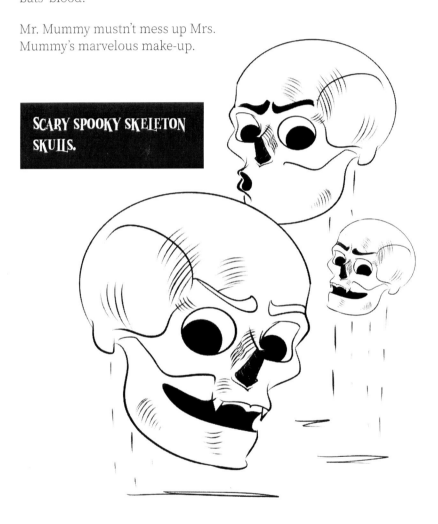

SCARY SPOOKY SKELETON SKULLS.

HALLOWEEN JOKES
FUN HALLOWEEN JOKES AND RIDDLES FOR KIDS, ENTERTAINMENT AND GIGGLES!

20

Plump pigs pick plump pumpkins.

Seven sinister stepsisters sewed sweaty skeleton sweaters.

Ghosts and goblins gaze at giggly girls.

Funny, funky Frankenstein funded his fun.

Frankly, Frankfurters fried in fish fat taste fresh and fine to Frankenstein.

HAUNTED HOUSES ON HALLOWEEN HAVE HAIR-RISING HORRIBLE HORRIFYING HAUNTS.

HALLOWEEN JOKES
FUN HALLOWEEN JOKES AND RIDDLES FOR KIDS, ENTERTAINMENT AND GIGGLES!

21

CHAPTER 4
FUNNY QUESTION AND ANSWER JOKES

Q. Why are skeletons always so calm?

Nothing can get under their skin.

Q. Why did the headless horseman start his own business?

He wanted to get ahead in life.

Q. Why aren't mummies more popular?

They're too wrapped up in themselves to worry about anyone else.

Q. WHAT HAPPENS WHEN YOU MEET A VAMPIRE SNOWMAN? YOU GET FROSTBITE.

Q. What does a ghost pick out of his nose?

Boo-gers.

Q. Why do ghosts diet?

They want to keep their ghoulish figures.

Q. What do ghost pandas eat?

Bam-Boo!

Q. What is a ghost's favorite play?

Romeo and Ghoul-iet.

Q. Why are monsters banned from the witch school?

They can't spell.

Q. What do skeletons order when they go to a restaurant?

Spare ribs.

Q. What keeps skeletons from playing music in church?

They have no organs.

Q. WHAT DO YOU CALL A WITCH AT THE BEACH? A SAND-WITCH.

HALLOWEEN JOKES
FUN HALLOWEEN JOKES AND RIDDLES FOR KIDS, ENTERTAINMENT AND GIGGLES!

23

Q. What happened when the witch got angry while on her broom?

She flew off the handle.

Q. How does a monster style her hair?

With scare-spray.

Q. What do you call a witch with a rash?

An itchy witchy.

Q. What do you call a pumpkin that helps people cross the road?

A crossing gourd.

Q. Why don't zombie pirates have any friends?

They're too salty.

Q. What do you call a zombie that's asleep?

The sleepwalking dead.

Q. Why can't cops arrest ghosts?

They can't be brought in alive.

Q. What do you call a zombie romance film?

A zom-com.

Q. What day of the week are ghosts the most scary?

Fright-Day.

Q. What do ghosts with bad eyesight wear?

Spook-tacles.

Q. What day of the week are zombies the loudest?

Moan-day.

Q. What happened to the monster that ate his house?

He got homesick.

Q. What does the witch's cereal sound like?

Snap, cackle, and pop.

Q. How do ghosts get from floor to floor in buildings?

They use the scare-case.

Q. What type of coffee does a vampire drink?

Coffin-ated.

Q. How does a witch in a hurry travel?

On a vroom-stick.

Q. Did you hear about the dirty graveyard?

You wouldn't want to be caught dead in there.

Q. What do you get when you cross a vampire with a college professor?

Blood tests.

HALLOWEEN JOKES
FUN HALLOWEEN JOKES AND RIDDLES FOR KIDS, ENTERTAINMENT AND GIGGLES!

24

Q. How do monsters keep cool in the summer?

They use the scare conditioner.

Q. Why do ghosts hate water?

It dampens their spirits.

Q. What did the ghost ask the twin witches?

Which witch is which?

Q. How do spirits wash their hair?

With sham-boo.

Q. What kind of dog does Dracula own?

A Bloodhound.

Q. What kind of cheese do scary creatures put on their pizza?

Monsterella cheese.

Q. How many witches does it take to change a lightbulb?

Just one, but she changes the bulb into a frog.

Q. WHAT IS A GHOST'S FAVORITE FRUIT?
BOO BERRIES.

HALLOWEEN JOKES
FUN HALLOWEEN JOKES AND RIDDLES FOR KIDS, ENTERTAINMENT AND GIGGLES!

25

Q. What is a spirit's favorite sports position?

The ghoul-keeper.

Q. How do you know if a vampire likes baseball?

See if he turns into a bat.

Q. What is a zombie's favorite street?

A dead end.

Q. Why was the crypt so loud?

Because of all the coffin!

Q. WHICH MONSTER IS THE LIFE OF THE PARTY?
THE BOOGIE MAN.

Q. What happens when you go on a date with a vampire?

You experience love at first bite.

Q. What is a spider's hobby?

Fly fishing.

Q. WHAT ROOM OF A HOUSE IS A GHOST UNABLE TO GO INTO? THE LIVING ROOM.

HALLOWEEN JOKES
FUN HALLOWEEN JOKES AND RIDDLES FOR KIDS, ENTERTAINMENT AND GIGGLES!

27

CHAPTER 5
HALLOWEEN RIDDLES

A man goes out at night for a drink. He stays out until the early hours of the morning but no matter how much he downs, he never gets a hangover. His favorite beverage is familiar, but rarely consumed by the general public. It is mostly served directly from the source, warm and fresh. The man can't survive without it and he's a sucker for a free drink, so he will never consider stopping his addiction. What does this man drink?

He's a vampire and drinks blood.

In the dark, late at night,
I float around and give a fright.
I'm a shadow of the living, and a specter of the dead.
People fear me when they are lying alone in their bed.
I float, I wail, and move through walls. I like to use your sheets.

What am I?

A ghost.

You are trapped in a haunted house with two friends for the night. A sudden storm overtakes the creepy home. All the power is out and there is no way to escape the house. You and your friends need to find a way to keep warm or you will all die. You search the entire haunted home and you and your friends find three stoves! One coal stove, one wood stove, and one gas stove—but you only have one match. What should you light first in order to survive the night?

Light the match first.

The maker has no need for it. The buyer probably won't use it. The user tends not to care about it.

What is it?

A casket.

HALLOWEEN JOKES
FUN HALLOWEEN JOKES AND RIDDLES FOR KIDS, ENTERTAINMENT AND GIGGLES!

28

A man is shot in the heart.
Nobody tries to save him and it
doesn't kill him. What happened?

He was shot after he was already
dead.

I protect and I stand tall.
Above the stalks, my purpose is to
strike fear in all.

What am I?

A scarecrow.

I don't have lungs, but I need air.
The more I eat, the more I grow.
I'm always hungry, ready to eat.
I'm rarely thirsty, I can barely
drink.
Shoot me, stab me, I don't mind.
But, suffocate or drown me and I
will die.

What am I?

Fire.

Ancient knowledge few can know,
in the night is where I roam.
Vermin I grab in my holy flight,
no one can hide from my sight.

An owl.

I am different sizes, shapes and
colors.
Many can see my veins.
I don't go inside.
The trees are where I reside.
If I fall to the ground, I will surely
die.

What am I?

A leaf.

With pointed fangs, I sit and wait.
With piercing force, I deal out fate.
Over bloodless victims, I display
my might.
I can forever join with just one bite.

What am I?

Dracula, or a stapler.

HALLOWEEN JOKES
FUN HALLOWEEN JOKES AND RIDDLES FOR KIDS, ENTERTAINMENT AND GIGGLES!

29

Darkness, dust, cobwebs and creaking floors,
secrets, spirits, strange noises and occasional slamming doors.

What am I?

A haunted house.

In this place people lie and people cry, and all ask why?
In this place where the people sleep and the people weep,
forever solitude they will keep.

What is this place?

A graveyard or cemetery.

I have a name but it is not mine.
You will not think about me while in your prime,
but people cry when I enter their sight.
While others will lie with me all day and night.

What am I?

A tombstone.

You're in a room with a ghost in it, but you are alone in the room. How is this true?

You are the ghost.

You may see me by the light of a bright round moon.
You can run but I will likely catch you soon.
You can hope for an escape with the rising sun.
But you have a better chance with silver bullets and a gun.

What am I?

A werewolf.

What's big, scary, and moves around on three wheels?

A monster riding a tricycle.

HALLOWEEN JOKES
FUN HALLOWEEN JOKES AND RIDDLES FOR KIDS, ENTERTAINMENT AND GIGGLES!

30

Each morning I appear at your feet. All day I follow, no matter how fast you run. Yet, I almost die in the midday sun. What am I?

A shadow.

Why can't a woman living in Florida be buried in Mexico?

You don't bury the living.

A rich man lived alone in a small cottage. Being handicapped, he had everything delivered to his cottage. One Friday, the mailman delivered a letter when he noticed that the front door was open. Through the opening, he could see the man's body lying in a pool of dried blood. When a police officer arrived, he investigated the area. On the porch were two bottles of curdled milk, Tuesday's newspaper, a catalog, flyers, and a stack of unopened mail. The police officer deemed it a crime scene and had a suspect in mind. Who did he suspect and how does he know?

The newspaper delivery person is the suspect. The absence of Wednesday and Thursday's newspaper points to the fact that the delivery person knew there was no one there to read it.

Poor people have it. Rich people need it. If you eat it, you will die. What is it?

Nothing.

I am in the present, but also in the past. I am wrapped, but not as a gift. I am named after a parent's name, but have no children with me. What am I?

A mummy.

22. I have a body, arms, legs and a head, but I'm heartless and have no guts. What am I?

A skeleton.

HALLOWEEN JOKES
FUN HALLOWEEN JOKES AND RIDDLES FOR KIDS, ENTERTAINMENT AND GIGGLES!

31

I hang upside down. I fly through the night. I love dark places but I don't have good eyesight. What am I?

A bat.

I'm tall when I'm young but I'm short when I'm old. Once every year, I make big pumpkins come alight. What am I?

A candle.

I always leave a trace behind me, so you can see where I've been. I have many extra legs, and some people scream at my sight. What am I?

A spider.

Frankenstein's father has three sons. One is named Snap, the second, Crackle. What is the third son's name?

Frankenstein.

Mrs. Jones had less than twenty pieces of candy left to give to trick or treaters for the night. She wanted to give it all away without eating any. Two trick or treaters arrived at the house and she wanted to share the treats evenly between the two, but when she tried to do it, there was still one piece left over. A third trick or treater arrived at the scene, so Mrs. Jones decided she would split the candy between all three of them. However, when she tried to share them equally, there was still one treat left in the bag. At last, a fourth trick or treater arrived and Mrs. Jones tried to split the treats between all four of the children. Yet again, she still had one treat left over! How many pieces of candy did Mrs. Jones have?

HALLOWEEN JOKES
FUN HALLOWEEN JOKES AND RIDDLES FOR KIDS, ENTERTAINMENT AND GIGGLES!

32

13 pieces of candy. 6 + 6 = 12, 4 + 4 + 4 =12, and 3 + 3 + 3 + 3 = 12. No matter how she splits it, Mrs. Jones will never be able to evenly disperse the candy unless 13 kids show up.

From the top of the head down to the tips of the toes, through every living animal I flow. Some people tend to faint when they see me outside, though! What am I?

Blood.

29. I'm the room in your house where you watch TV and have your fun, but I am also the one room in which dead things will never, ever come. What room am I?

The living room.

A group of monsters are having a foot race. The monster in third place passes the monster in second place. What place is he now?

In second place.

Why don't mummies go on summer vacations?

They're scared to relax and unwind.

I am known to bring bad luck and be a bit dark, but one thing is for sure, you will never hear me bark. What am I?

A black cat.

Dracula loves to draw this, as well as, put it in the bank. What is it?

Blood.

34. What is lifeless, cold, stiff, and surrounds a graveyard?

A fence.

HALLOWEEN JOKES
FUN HALLOWEEN JOKES AND RIDDLES FOR KIDS, ENTERTAINMENT AND GIGGLES!

33

What is wicked, white, spooky, and goes up and down?

A ghost stuck in an elevator.

What is red, juicy, and delicious but could be poisonous if it comes from the wrong person?

Snow White's apple.

No matter what type you are, who you are, or where you are,

when I'm thirsty I will come and find you. What am I?

A vampire.

There is an old man with a white beard that performs feats of magic and is forgotten around Halloween, who is he?

Santa Claus.

39. What can be sweet, sour, soft, hard, or chewy all at once?

Candy.

I am decorated with flair one day a year, and the center of attention even when you make me into dessert. What am I?

A pumpkin.

41. Where do you find Benjamin Franklin, George Washington, Abraham Lincoln, and Thomas Jefferson?

In the cemetery.

Ghosts, goblins, witches, and vampires always come searching for me on a dark autumn night. With a ding and a buzz, they impatiently wait with open arms for me. What am I?

Halloween candy.

HALLOWEEN JOKES
FUN HALLOWEEN JOKES AND RIDDLES FOR KIDS, ENTERTAINMENT AND GIGGLES!

34

I have thousands of ears. I listen every night. I can't hear a thing, not even a fright. What am I?

A cornfield.

What's the problem with identical twin witches?

You never know which witch is which.

How do you spell candy with two letters?

C and Y.

I have a head but no body. I can cause a fright, but my smile lights up the night. What am I?

A jack-o'-lantern.

What goes "Ha, ha, ha"—THUD?

A zombie laughing his head off.

Night and day my bones are pale. What am I?

A skeleton.

It is Halloween night and your friends dare you to go into a creepy old house. You sneak up to the door, a little afraid and wondering what is waiting for you. You enter the door and you see a long hallway leading into a dark room with three doors. You're kind of terrified inside this place. You turn back to get back outside, but the door is closed and locked. You scream for help but there is no response. You can't see very well, so you look for a light source. You find a light switch and flip it on. There is no power in the house. You are still terrified but can only follow the hallway to the three doors.

HALLOWEEN JOKES
FUN HALLOWEEN JOKES AND RIDDLES FOR KIDS, ENTERTAINMENT AND GIGGLES!

35

You're grabbed and told you must choose a door. Behind one door is a bottomless pit that you will have to jump in. Behind the second door is an electric chair which you must sit in, and behind the last door is a pool filled with acid which you would have to swim in. Which door should you choose to go through?

The electric chair. If the power is out, the chair can't be turned on. It's the only safe choice.

I am wrapped up but am not a gift, I am kept neatly in a chamber and when people find me, I am a great treasure. What am I?

A mummy.

If the witch has a black cat for a companion, and a jack-o'-lantern has a candle, what does a vampire have to keep him company?

A bloodhound.

Oz had a good one from the north, and one from the south, but wicked ones in the east and in the west.
However, flying around on a broomstick,
is how I'm known the best.

What am I?

A witch.

I'm made out of different body parts,
and brought to life by electricity.
There are bolts in my neck and I have green skin.
Why can't anyone show me some pity?

Who am I?

Frankenstein's monster.

HALLOWEEN JOKES
FUN HALLOWEEN JOKES AND RIDDLES FOR KIDS, ENTERTAINMENT AND GIGGLES!

36

I walk around aimlessly although I am dead,
I like to eat the brains right out of your head.

What am I?

A zombie.

Often buried with silver and gold,
I'm an undead creature all wrapped up in myself.

What am I?

A mummy.

This is a common little thing,
That a lot of people fear.
The fear has a name,
arachnophobia.

What am I?

A spider.

It is thanks to me,
that you can sweep your floor.
I'm also used by the witches that be,
so they can fly and soar.

What am I?

A broomstick.

Eye of newt and toe of frog?
Just a spot inside this big black pot.

What is it?

A cauldron.

Two friends sat down for a meal. They both ordered iced tea. One of the friends drank several teas and was fine, but the other sipped on one drink and died. All drinks were poisoned. How did one friend survive?

The ice was poisoned. The friend that drank quickly never let the ice melt.

HALLOWEEN JOKES
FUN HALLOWEEN JOKES AND RIDDLES FOR KIDS, ENTERTAINMENT AND GIGGLES!

37

What do all the mummies, zombies, vampires, goblins and witches have in common?

The letter 'i.'

61. Often used by witches to cast their spells,
I am a slimy thing, and ugly as well.

What am I?

A toad.

They call me Jack.
I have a head, but a body I lack.

What am I?

A jack-o'-lantern.

Why are there fences around graveyards?

Because people are dying to get in.

Read or write me, I'm always good for a fright.
I can be fun and spooky, and I'm best told at night.

What am I?

A scary story.

I am friend to one, fiend to another.
I am silky smooth and make people dance when they touch me.

What am I?

A spider-web.

I'm a vampire's greatest fear,
But one of a chef's favorite ingredients.

What am I?

Garlic.

The more you take of me, the more I multiply. What am I?

Footsteps.

I am scary and spooky. When you have more of me you will see less of everything. What am I?

Darkness.

Look in my face and I am somebody. Look into my back and I am nobody. What am I?

A mirror.

HALLOWEEN JOKES
FUN HALLOWEEN JOKES AND RIDDLES FOR KIDS, ENTERTAINMENT AND GIGGLES!

39

CONCLUSION

Did some of these jokes and riddles give you real moans and groans—or did you find them to be super stinky like zombie armpits? Either way, we hope those Halloween jokes gave you a good giggle! These Halloween jokes are family friendly, and are guaranteed to make anyone laugh, no matter how old they are.

Although Halloween is celebrated in many different ways all over the world, everyone can appreciate a good and scary joke, riddle, or pun!

Halloween is a holiday where fun is key. What better way to bring the family together and have a good time than over a good joke? Feel free to tell them and share them throughout the Halloween season. Have a spooky fun time!

We also hope you enjoyed the selection of poems and interesting facts. Tell your friends and family these and you'll be the star of the party!

REFERENCES

12 spooky facts you never knew about Halloween. (2016 October 13). Orchid Republic Floral Boutique. https:// orchidrepublic.com/blogs/news/12-spooky-facts-you-never-knew-about-halloween.

Banya, D. (2016 October 17). 48 spooktacularly funny Halloween jokes for kids. Danyabanya.com. https://www. danyabanya.com/spooky-jokes-kids/.

Betinah. (2021 October 29). Halloween tongue twisters. Garden Players. https://gardenplayers.com/2021/10/ halloween-tongue-twisters/.

Coleridge, M.A. (2022). The witch. Academy of American Poets. https://poets.org/poem/witch.

Dunbar, P.L. (n.d.). The Haunted Oak by. Poetry Foundation. Retrieved May 9, 2022, from https://www. poetryfoundation.org/poems/44195/the-haunted-oak.

Field, E. (n.d.). The night wind. Holyjoe.org. Retrieved May 9, 2022, from

http://holyjoe.org/poetry/field2.htm.

Funny Halloween jokes and tongue twisters for kids. (2012 September 7). Kids Play and Create. https://www. kidsplayandcreate.com/funny-halloween-jokes-and-tongue-twisters-for-kids/

Halloween: Halloween tongue twisters. (n.d.). American Folklore. Retrieved April 27, 2022, from https:// americanfolklore.net/folklore/2009/08/spooky_tongue_twisters.html.

Halloween jokes: Puns. (n.d.). Halloweenjokes.com. Retrieved April 27, 2022, from https://halloweenjokes. com/?s=Puns.

Halloween poems for kids. (n.d.). Family Fun. Retrieved May 9, 2022, from https://www.familyfun.ie/halloween-poems/.

Halloween Tongue Twisters. (n.d.). Bamboozle. Retrieved April 27, 2022, from https://www.baamboozle.com/ game/205815.

Halloween trivia: 13 facts about the 1978 slasher. (n.d.). Geek Soup. Retrieved May 9, 2022, from https:// geeksoup.co.uk/halloween-13-things-you-didnt-know/.

The history of Milk Duds candy. (n.d.). Hershyland. Retrieved May 9, 2022, from https://www.hersheyland.com/ milk-duds.

Liles, M. (2021 October 2). 75 hilarious Halloween riddles for a spooky, silly good time. Parade. https://parade. com/1258849/marynliles/halloween-riddles/.

Ludlam, J. (2021 June 10). 106 laugh-out-loud Halloween jokes that'll tickle a skeleton's funny bone. Country Living. https://www.countryliving.com/entertaining/a32963261/halloween-jokes/.

Maci. (2022 February 14). Halloween facts. Facts.net. https://facts.net/halloween-facts/.

Maria. (2007 October 25). Halloween tongue twisters for the classroom. Pension Sprachschule Maria Shipley. http://www.pension-sprachschule.de/general/halloween-tongue-twisters-for-the-classroom/.

McDonough, L.S., Picard, C. (2021 October 29). Good Housekeeping. https://www.goodhousekeeping.com/ holidays/halloween-ideas/a35150/halloween-facts/

HALLOWEEN JOKES
FUN HALLOWEEN JOKES AND RIDDLES FOR KIDS, ENTERTAINMENT AND GIGGLES!

41

O'Sullivan, K., & Donovan, B. (2021 October 27). 90 funny Halloween puns that'll give all your ghoul friends a good cackle. Country Living. https://www.countryliving.com/life/a23012541/halloween-puns-funny-cute/.

Parris, J. (2021 August 12). These 25 knock knock jokes for kids are frightfully funny. Romper. https://www.romper.com/life/halloween-knock-knock-jokes.

Poe, E.A. (n.d.). The raven. Poetry Foundation. Retrieved May, 9, 2022, from https://www.poetryfoundation.org/poems/48860/the-raven.

Reese, W. (2019 October 23). Verify: Is it illegal to wear Halloween masks in Dublin if you're 16 or older? 13WMAZ. https://www.13wmaz.com/article/news/verify/verify-halloween-masks-in-dublin/93-794bbfca-06ec-42bd-b1a1-956ed2544803.

Shakespeare, W. (n.d.). Song of the witches: "Double, double toil and trouble." Poetry Foundation. Retrieved May 9, 2022, from https://www.poetryfoundation.org/poems/43189/song-of-the-witches-double-double-toil-and-trouble.

Simmons, A. (2021 October 27). Trick or treat! You need to learn these 20 corny Halloween jokes. Reader's Digest Canada. Retrieved April 27, 2022, from https://www.readersdigest.ca/culture/corny-halloween-jokes/.

Social media influencing near-record Halloween spending. (2019 September 25). National Retail Federation. https://nrf.com/media-center/press-releases/social-media-influencing-near-record-halloween-spending.

Su, C.S. (2012 October 29). Halloween tongue twisters. Prezi. https://prezi.com/umq_qu-asaca/halloween-tongue-twisters/.

Synan, M. (2018 August 22). What is bobbing for apples? History. https://www.history.com/news/what-is-bobbing-for-apples.

Tripple, M. (2020 September 23). The funniest Halloween knock knock jokes EverythingMom. https://www.everythingmom.com/jokes-for-kids/halloween-knock-knock-jokes.

LET'S
GROW
TOGETHER!

Made in United States
North Haven, CT
20 September 2023

41786453R00026